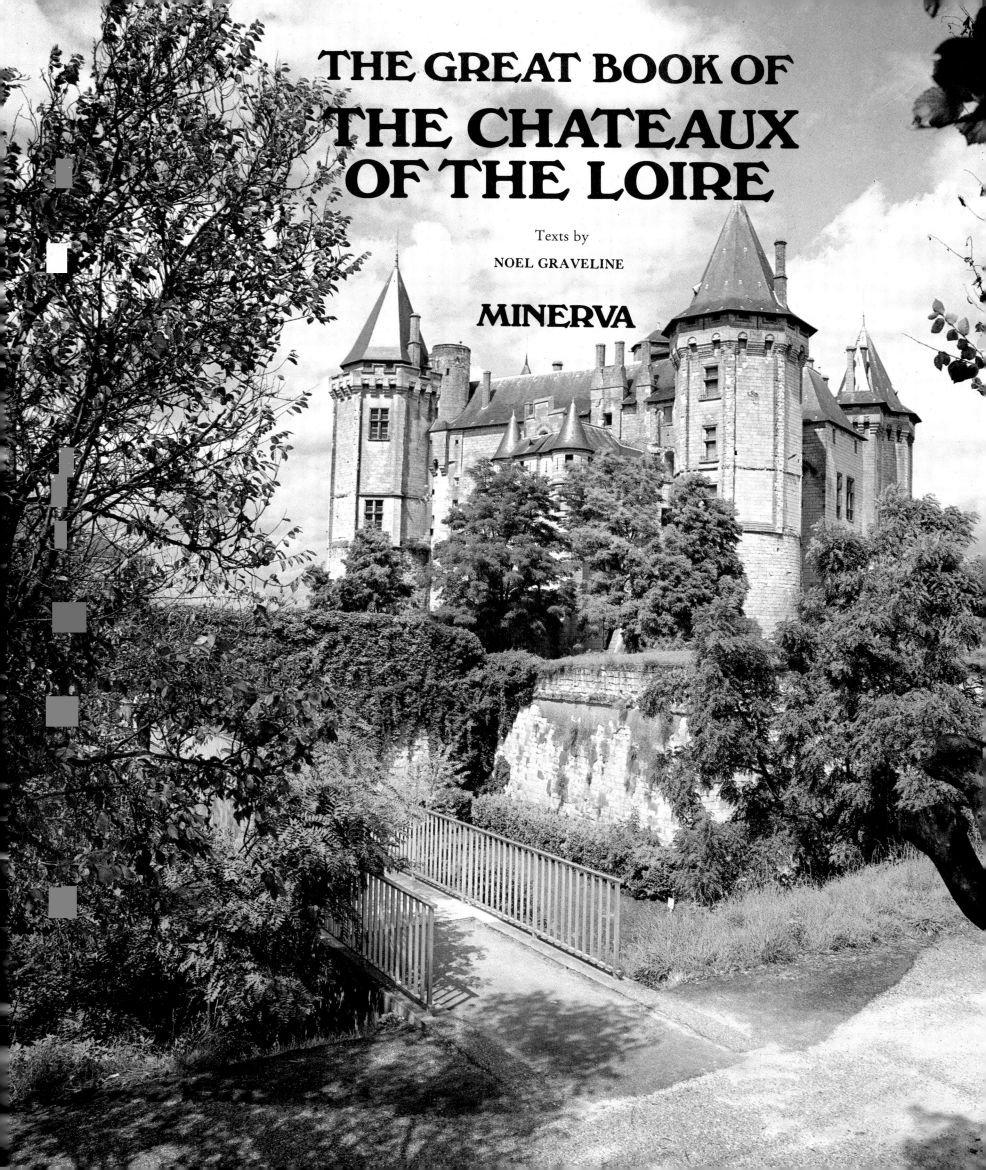

THE GREAT BOOK OF
THE CHATEAUX
OF THE LOIRE

Texts by

NOEL GRAVELINE

MINERVA

© Editions Minerva SA,
Genève-Paris, 1987

ISBN 2-8307-0000-7
Printed in Italy

Cover: the Château of Azay-le-Rideau. *Fly leaves:* detail from the façade of the Château of Amboise. *Title page:* the Château of Saumur.

These two pages: this fireplace in the Château of Blois (1) is adorned with the emblem of Louis XII, the porcupine. Detail from the façade of the Château of Azay-le-Rideau (2). The royal emblem in the Château of Blois (3). Gothic windows at Châteaudun (4). door at Langeais (5).

The map labels (Loire Valley châteaux):

Laval (p. 144), Le Mans, Châteaudun (p. 6), Montargis, Orléans, Craon (p. 143), Courtanvaux (p. 143), Meung-sur-Loire (p. 113), Châteauneuf-sur-Loire (p. 113), Poncé-sur-le-Loir (p. 143), Lavardin (p. 114), Vendôme (p. 120), Talcy (p. 8), Les Briottières (p. 137), Bazouges-sur-le-Loir (p. 143), Gallerande (p. 143), La Possonnière (p. 118), Beaugency (p. 113), Sully-sur-Loire (p. 4), Gien (p. 4), Le Plessis-Bourré (p. 110), Durtal (p. 140), La Flèche, Le Lude (p. 111), La Roche-Racan (p. 134), Château-Renault (p. 128), Ménars (p. 116), Chantecaille (p. 116), Chambord (p. 10), Le Plessis-Macé (p. 140), Baugé (p. 136), Vaujours (p. 135), Blois (p. 20), Villesavin (p. 120), Blancafort (p. 122), Montgeoffroy (p. 98), Beauregard (p. 28), Cheverny (p. 28), Troussay (p. 120), Serrant (p. 106), Angers (p. 102), Baudry (p. 130), Tours (p. 135), Chaumont-sur-Loire (p. 32), Fougère-sur-Bièvre (p. 114), La Verrerie (p. 123), Luynes (p. 66), Amboise (p. 56), Le Clos-Lucé (p. 65), Le Moulin (p. 36), La Ferté-Imbault (p. 127), Brissac-Quincé (p. 101), Cinq-Mars-la-Pile (p. 129), Langeais (p. 76), Villandry (p. 68), Plessis-lès-Tours (p. 67), Pagode de Chanteloup, Le Gué-Péan (p. 36), Romorantin, Béthune (p. 123), Boumois (p. 136), Les Réaux (p. 127), Montrichard (p. 116), Boucard (p. 122), Saumur (p. 96), Chanzeaux (p. 138), Azay-le-Rideau (p. 72), Saché (p. 134), Leugny (p. 130), Chenonceau (p. 49), Selles-sur-Cher (p. 40), Vierzon, Le Pont-de-Varenne (p. 98), Ussé (p. 82), Montbazon (p. 132), Montpoupon (p. 42), Saint-Aignan (p. 38), Le Coudray-Montbault (p. 138), Montsoreau (p. 94), Chinon (p. 87), Montrésor (p. 42), Villentrois (p. 127), Valençay (p. 39), Bourges, La Tremblaye (p. 141), Montreuil-Bellay (p. 90), Le Coudray-Montpensier (p. 129), Loches (p. 44), Genillé (p. 129), Le Rivau (p. 132), Bridoré (p. 128), Argy (p. 124), Issoudun, Le Châtellier-le-Fort (p. 130), Le Grand-Pressigny (p. 130), Châtellerault, La Guerche (p. 130), Azay-le-Ferron (p. 124), Châteauroux, St Amand-Montrond, Poitiers, Le Blanc, Sarzay (p. 127), La Châtre, Château-Guillaume (p. 124)

Rivers/regions: MAINE, ANJOU, TOURAINE, SOLOGNE, BERRY, Loire, Loir, Sarthe, Mayenne, Oudon, Layon, Vienne, Indre, Cher, Creuse, Gartempe, Clain, Manse, Indrois, Beuvron, Sauldre, Yèvre, Auron, Sèvre Nantaise, Thouet

0 10 20 50 km

◁ 4

5 ▷

Gien

Traditionally, Gien has always marked the point at which the Loire begins its stately progress past the succession of regal châteaux which have made the river famous the world over. The town's importance is emphasized by the legend according to which Charlemagne himself founded the castle which originally gave birth to Gien. The present large château which, with its two wings of brick and its slate roofs, dominates the town, was built by Anne de Beaujeu, Countess of Gien.

It was she who — serving as a perfectly exemplary Regent at the end of the 15th century — gave further proof of her talents; this most worthy woman, known to her subjects as *Madame la Grande*, left behind her a château whose sober beauty derives simply from the rhythm of dual-colored bricks and ties of white stone. It now houses the International Museum of Hunting, which itself enhances the elegance of the superbly proportioned rooms with its remarkable tapestries, a number of rare exhibits and hundreds of trophies which at once bring to mind the nearby Sologne, an area richly blessed with game.

The Château of Gien houses the International Museum of Hunting: here, the Great Hall (1). Two other exhibition halls in the museum (2 and 3). View of the château (4). The Château of Sully-sur-Loire with its moats (5).

Sully-sur-Loire

In a commanding location, overlooking a bend in the river, with a history that can be traced all the way back to the early Middle Ages, Sully-sur-Loire has an even more defensive character than Gien. Apart from Joan of Arc, who escaped from it to keep up the fight against the English, the château's principal claim to fame is Maximilien de Béthune, a great Frenchman who is known to history only by the name of his place of residence, as Duke of Sully. It is he who was responsible for the majesty of the buildings and grounds, as he retired to Sully after the assassination of Henri IV to live the life of a prince. He diverted the Loire away from the château walls, dug moats supplied with water from the smaller river Sange, laid out the park and expanded the buildings, where his apartments can still be seen.

In this way he gave the ancient fortress with its round towers — a major innovation by the architect Raymond du Temple in 1387 — the serene and majestic air which it has retained to this day. The interior is equally impressive. The beams, made of the heart of the chestnut tree, are the most remarkable specimens of medieval timberwork still surviving; they probably served as the upper gallery for the plays which Voltaire, banished from Paris by the Regent of his day, performed with his urbane troupe of actors.

△ 4

1 △

5 ▷

2 ◁

3 ▷

Châteaudun

The first of the châteaux of the Loire that one comes to on the way from Paris is Châteaudun, which towers above the Loir (a river which flows into the Sarthe near Angers) from a height of 200 feet, in a protective position at the border of the Beauce region. The old feudal fort, which had been owned by the Orléans family since 1391, was symbolized by the circular keep. In the 15th century it was replaced by the Dunois wing and the Sainte-Chapelle, to which the Longueville wing was added in the Renaissance. The counterforts of their foundations form a soaring mass, perched precipitously above the river, whereas the courtyard side is of the utmost delicacy, enhanced by three characteristic staircases. These had been preceded in the medieval period by a simple spiral hidden inside a tower. The advent of the Gothic style brought high flamboyant bay windows, while the noble harmony of loggias with surbased vaults was a product of the Renaissance.

The interior of this bright and comfortable residence has been well preserved, its most notable feature being the huge kitchens, whose palm-tree vaults repose on three monumental fireplaces. Some interesting Flemish and Parisian tapestries, as well as furniture of the 17th and 18th centuries, are on display in the rooms on the ground floor. The Sainte-Chapelle, which was built for Dunois, the famous bastard son of Louis d'Orléans, also contains some important historical pieces, such as the fresco of the Last Supper, or the fifteen polychrome statues place there by Dunois himself.

The Château of Châteaudun (1). The original kitchens (2), the drawing-room in the Dunois wing (3) and a fireplace (4). The château on the courtyard side, with the keep and the chapel (5).

4 ▽

5 ▷

Talcy

This discreet château of the 15th and 16th centuries owes its place in history to the literary memories with which it is associated: it was bought in 1517 by the cousin of Catherine de Médicis, Bernard de Salviati, whose daughter Cassandre inspired the poet Ronsard, while his niece Diana later seduced another poet, Agrippa d'Aubigné. Much later still, the family kept its literary tradition alive by giving birth to Alfred de Musset. However, the Château of Talcy has charms of its own, because its rather austere appearance is offset by two small wonders which it contains: a period dovecote and a winepress which has been in working order for the past four hundred years.

Talcy. An original 17th-century winepress, still in working order (1). A 17th-century bedroom (2). The great 18th-century drawing-room (3). The courtyard of the château (4).

Chambord

"Just like a woman with her hair blowing in the wind", was how Chateaubriand described the contrast between the serenity of the façades of Chambord and its endless array of bristling superstructures. The name of the architectural genius who built this gigantic palace on the orders of François I is not known, though there is good reason to

suppose that Leonardo da Vinci, who died in 1519, just as construction was beginning, may have had something to do with the design of those façades, which are all influenced by the golden number. One wonders whether the king, who was passionately fond of hunting, chose this location near the Forest of Boulogne, or whether the amorous side of his nature predominated, an account of his interest in some nearby titled lady. Whatever the reason for his choice, this setting inspired him to build a veritable residential fortress, complete with towers and a colossal keep which the Renaissance, at its height, transformed into a sumptuous palace. Only Versailles, a century later, succeeded in surpassing Chambord. Above the 365 chimneys which form the "hair" Chateaubriand found so appealing, stands the lantern and its majestic sculpted fleur-de-lys, the crowning glory of the Great Staircase which is the most striking feature of the château.

Ornamental detail from the front of the Château of Chambord (1). The façade of the château seen from the nearby river (2). The main façade and the Porte Royale (3).

Located in the very heart of the palace, it leads to the four guard rooms by two superimposed spirals entwined around an empty stairwell: in this way two visitors can ascend the steps without losing sight of each other, but without meeting until they reach the famous terraces and their chimneys, superbly embellished with slates cut into the form of medallions. As a tangle of nooks and crannies highly conducive to intrigue and flirtation, or as an incomparable vantage-point from which one could watch the parades or the return of the hunt, these terraces played an essential role in the life of the court.

François I died before construction could be completed, but he made a point of residing and entertaining at Chambord; he even invited Emperor Charles V, who was deeply impressed. Henri II continued his father's work by building the two lattice staircases at the corners of the court-yard. Thereafter, however, the monarchy moved away from Chambord, except for hunting expeditions in the nearby forests. Louis XIII took a renewed interest in the château which he had ceded to his brother; indeed La Grande Demoiselle, his brother's daughter, made her confession of love to Lauzun in one of the drawing rooms at Chambord. The Crown returned to the château

Chambord. The château seen at different times of the day and during different seasons of the year.

◁ 1   2 △   3 ▽

with Louis XIV, for whom Molière staged two of his plays there. During the first performance of *Monsieur de Pourceaugnac,* noting with alarm the king's unsmiling face, the composer Lully is said to have jumped from the stage onto and through the harpsichord, to howls of royal laugther.

Louis XV awarded Chambord to his exiled father-in-law Stanislas Leczinski, who regrettably decided to fill in the moats. There was one final restoration of the château's former splendor, with Marshal Maurice de Saxe, who had been rewarded for his victory at Fontenoy in a truly regal manner; during his tenure, the whole estate resounded to the sound of trumpets and the thundering hooves of his regiments of Tartars. The marshal was eventually killed in a duel by his rival, the Prince de Conti. Then, abandoned, and narrowly escaping destruction at the hands of the Revolution, the Château of Chambord succeeded in recovering its splendor only because it was bought by the State in 1930. Although it is not filled with sumptuous furniture, it does nonetheless show the visitor one of the most refined stone decors produced by the early Renaissance.

Chambord. The Great Staircase (1). One of the guard rooms and the ornamental salamanders on the ceiling vaults (2 and 3).

15

1 △

2 ▽

Chambord. The Hall of the Suns (1). The apartments of Louis XIV (2). The royal bedroom (3). A view of the surrounding countryside (4). The château's spectacular lanterns and chimneys (5). *Following pages:* general view of the château.

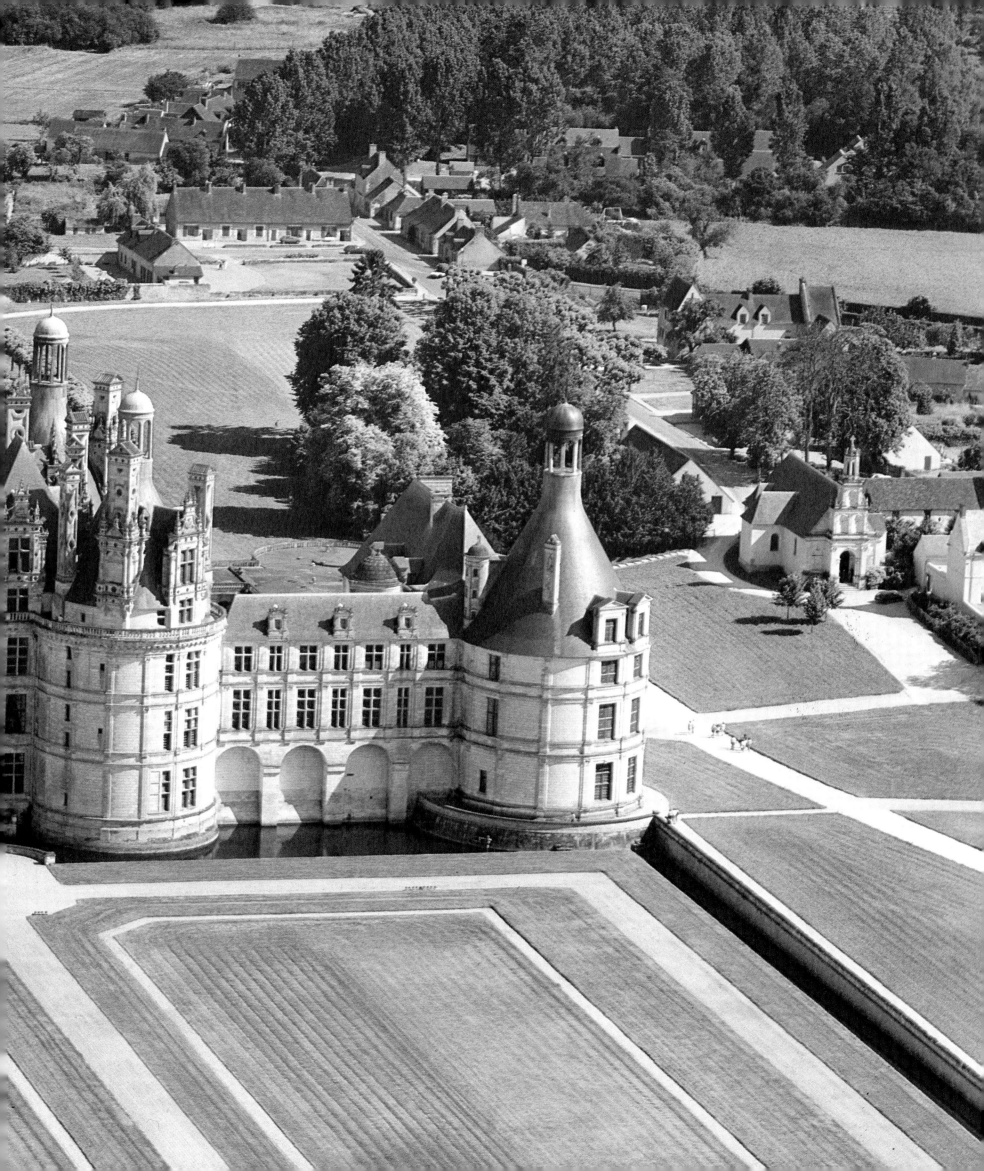

Blois

Above the "stairway of streets" of the old town, to use Victor Hugo's phrase, the Château of Blois provides an illustration of all the French architectural styles, from the Gothic pointed arch to the flowering of classicism. Its oldest section, beneath the sharply pointed and windowless roof, contains the superb Chamber of States (Chambre des Etats), which was a part of the medieval castle built here probably by Thibault IV, Count of Blois, who was

take a look at the buildings erected by Louis XII which extend to the other side of this original section.

As soon as he ascended the throne, the king, who had been born at Blois, set about converting the fortress into a comfortable and suitably dignified residence. This wing is a very graceful asymmetrical structure, much enhanced by the mixed colors of brick and stone which frame each opening; it is flanked by two square towers containing

also responsible for the Cathedral of Chartres. Henri III twice assembled the States General of the Kingdom in this exceedingly pure Gothic setting; but the deed for which he is most remembered in connection with Blois is the assassination of the Duke of Guise. The ambush in which Scarface was cut down, on the king's orders, took place on the second floor of the François I wing, which is renowned for its splendid octagonal staircase, the pride and glory of Blois. Seen from the middle of the inner courtyard, this wing is situated to the left of the old castle; however, one would do well to

spiral staircases, while the various rooms of this royal manor are connected by a gallery resting on basket-handle arches. The choir of the St. Calais chapel, whose spire can be seen above a low gallery, is also from the period of Louis XII; it marks the

The Francis I wing of the Château of Blois (1). Another view of the same wing and the grand staircase (2). The Façade des Loges (3).

beginning of the third side of the château, while at the same time leaving an opening to the escarpment and the Foix Tower, another vestige of the 13th century, overlooking the Loire.

The entrance to the château, located on the outer side of this Louis II wing, is adorned with a wealth of sculpture depicting not only the pomp of royalty but also the colorful and indeed spicy qualities of the lives of its former inhabitants. The king strikes a glorious pose in a flamboyant niche above the main entrance, astride a hack, using a now obsolete ambling step which at one time had to be learned laboriously. His curious emblem, the porcupine, occurs on the postern, while his Roman numeral is on the gable of one window, with the lily of France on the other. Anne of Brittany, the second of the three royal wives of the "Father of the People", is represented more discreetly on this wing of the château, in the form of an ermine and the letter "A", both finely carved. Among the

windows, which are arranged in a charmingly capricious pattern, the left balcony was for the use of the king, who used to come out onto it from his bedroom in the morning to consult with his minister, Cardinal d'Amboise, who lived in a nearby townhouse.

With a new king came a new emblem. Like the many other buildings which marked the various parts of his reign, the François I wing was adorned with the crowned salamander. Blois was his first venture, and on either side of the 13th-century ramparts he concentrated on remodeling older buildings, rather than on erecting any wholly original architecture. Nonetheless, this part of the

Blois. The Louis XII façade (1) and a detail of that same façade (2) with the statue of Louis XII (3).

3 ▷

château is the best of Blois, because only a dozen years after the death of Louis XII the Italian style, which could already be discerned beneath certain arabesques, fully came into its own precisely in this wing, being symbolized by the famous staircase which protrudes into the courtyard. This Renaissance masterpiece, which in the words of Balzac was "as elaborate as a Chinese ivory", has a lattice-pattern on five of its faces, thus making it possible for the court to watch the festivities of which the period was so fond, not only from the stands but also from the stairs.

The reason why François I showed such sollicitude for the château of Blois was that his wife, Claude de France, the daughter of Louis XII, was very happy there. The ermine which adorns the château walls was in fact the emblem of that young queen, whose untimely death occurred only a short time after the building was completed. The king's wholehearted support for the Renaissance did not preclude some indulgence in traditional French

fantasies, as can be seen from the asymmetrical arrangement of windows and skylights. The exterior façade was placed over the original ramparts, which François felt were not sufficiently open towards the town; the two stories of loggias with a row of gargoyles and a gallery above them are somewhat reminiscent of the Vatican; though here again Italianate style does not supplant French taste.

Some traces of the original design, such as fireplaces, door frames and sculpted decorative work, are still to be seen in the apartments of this wing, on the second floor. Here we find the Guard Room, scene of many balls, where Ronsard and Cassandre

Blois. The Queen's Apartments (1). The study of Catherine de Médicis, with secret compartments hidden behind its carved wood paneling (2). Her bedroom (3). The State Room (4). The Great Hall in the Louis XII wing (5).

4 ◁

5 ▷

once met; François I's small study, with its lavish wood paneling; and, on the gallery side, the bedroom where Catherine de Médicis died, less than two weeks after the château's most famous guest, forgotten and unlamented. That guest, of course, was the Duke of Guise, whose dramatic murder, on Christmas Eve 1588, still stirs the imagination. Blois contains abundant illustrations of this page in French history, done by 19th-century artists.

And that was really the end of the royal presence at the Château of Blois, as Henri IV and Louis XIII went there very rarely. After the incident in 1617, in which Marie de Médicis proved to be too heavy for the rope ladder she used in her escape from the château, Blois was bypassed by history. Gaston d'Orléans was awarded the château and made it his residence; the grand renovation projects which he commissioned Mansart to carry out were never completed, through lack of funds. The brother of Louis XIII never took advantage of the one residence he did build, between the François I wing and the nave of the St. Calais chapel, which was demolished on that occasion. It was fortunate indeed that Richelieu withheld funding from the prince, because this project would have required the elimination of the entire château; moreover, the classical patterns of the Gaston d'Orléans wing, despite all the talent of Mansart, cannot withstand comparison with the florid magnificence of the Renaissance. From the exterior, however, the majestic quality of this structure is most impressive, and the decor inspired by the architectural orders of Antiquity in no way detracts from the rest of the château, behind the foliage.

Therein lies the miraculous secret of the Château of Blois — so rich that it is impossible to describe it in detail, yet at the same time adorned with the beauty of simple things.

Blois. Detail from a fireplace in the study of Catherine de Médicis (1). Two ornaments depicting the salamander, the emblem of François I (2 and 4). The porcupine, which symbolized Louis XII, shown here with the "A" from the heraldic device of Anne of Brittany (3). Ornamental detail on a fireplace (5).

2 △

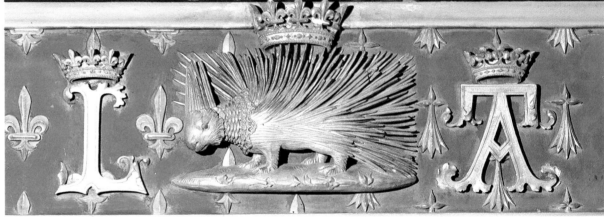

3 △

5 ▷

1
◁

4
▷

Cheverny

If one were asked to think of a château totally unlike Blois, Cheverny is the name that would come to mind. Erected without any interruption, well away from the Loire, between 1604 and 1634, the château has always belonged to the family after which it is named, and manifests a perfect unity of style, even in the living quarters, which contain one of the finest decorative ensembles of the reign of Louis XIII. And when the descendants of Hurault de Cheverny unleash their pack of seventy Anglo-French hounds for the hunt, it seems very much as if time has stood still for the last three and a half centuries at the edge of the Sologne.

For the visitor, Cheverny is a picture of flawless symmetry coupled with the majesty of a refined classicism. As soon as one has climbed the few steps leading into the château, one is dazzled by its magnificence: in the Grand Salon the painted decors and the giltwork are eclipsed by the precious furniture and paintings by Titian, Mignard or the studio of Raphael. The Petit Salon is decor- ated with five Flemish tapestries, while three adjacent rooms which are now once again open — a gallery, another drawing room and the library with its remarkable wood paneling — rival each other's splendor. The ground floor also includes the dining room, with its ceiling in the French style.

The lavishly sculpted Grand Staircase leads upstairs to the gem of Cheverny, after the Salle d'Armes, with its memories of war. The King's Bed- room is so regal as to deserve its title: in fact one hardly knows which to admire most — the tapes- tries, the Renaissance fireplace, the canopied bed with its Persian silks or the ceiling in the Italianate style.

Cheverny. The Trophy Room, in the outbuildings of the château (1). The Guard Room (2). The King's Bedroom (3). The façade of the château (4). *Following pages:* panoramic view of the château, with its park and flowerbeds.

2 △

1 ◁

3 ▷

28

4 △

Chaumont

Three passionate women, Diane de Poitiers, Madame de Staël and Madame Récamier left the imprint of their personalities on Chaumont, although this slightly grim, feudal-looking castle seems better suited to military adventures. A closer look behind the military trappings reveals some of the gentleness of the Renaissance; and all doubt is dispeled when one enters the inner courtyard and finds, on the site of a former wing of the fortress, a terrace with a most appealing residence.

However, Diane de Poitiers' decision to move to Chaumont was not taken with any great enthusiasm, but as a result of one of those curious turns which are so frequent in history, when her rival, Catherine de Médicis, "invited" her to swap Chenonceau for this more modest château. The living quarters thus comprise the bedrooms of the two enemies; but Diane could not bring herself to accept such a humiliation, and lived out her life at the delicate Château of Anet. The other famous women who lived here in the 19th century also must have associated Anet, to a greater or lesser degree, with the bitter taste of exile. Madame de Staël, whose fiery style had upset Napoleon, had to leave Paris, and found Chaumont sufficiently to her liking to move there, with her "court", including Benjamin Constant and Madame Récamier.

It is not until modern times that we encounter a more serene female occupant, the Princesse de Broglie, who was responsible for the magnificent ceramic tiles of the Salle du Conseil, the work of 17th-century Sicilian artists, which was brought from Palermo around 1900. The superb stables, which can still be visited today, were built by her husband slightly away from the main house.

Chaumont-sur-Loire. The main courtyard (1). The drawbridge and the two circular towers at the main entrance (2). The dining room (3). The château in its natural setting, overlooking the Loire (4). *Following pages:* the majesty of Chaumont.

1 △

2 △   3 ▽   4 ▷

Lassay

Deep in the heart of the Sologne, the Château du Moulin was built near Lassay for a gentleman who had been a companion of Charles VII in his youth. Philippe du Moulin, who had become a captain, saved his sovereign's life at the battle of Fornoue, in 1495: the château testifies to the pace of his advancement thereafter. These buildings, of lozenge-shaped bricks with stone ties, reflected in the water of the moats, are no longer those of a warrior, though they do not yet have quite the degree of refinement one finds in other lordly residences of the same period. Furnishings tyical of the Sologne about that time still exist in the keep.

Le Gué-Péan

This château, which was used as a hunting-lodge in the 16th and 17th centuries, is one of the least well-known in the whole of Touraine. Yet it has an imposing feudal layout, with four towers enclosing a courtyard and derives much charm from the assorted shapes of its roofs, its bay windows with pilasters and its succession of drawing rooms which contain a fine collection of tapestries and paintings.

The original period kitchens of the Château du Moulin (1) and its brick buildings, surrounded by moats (3). A room from the Château of Le Gué-Péan (2). The façade and formal courtyard, Gué-Péan (4 and 5).

3 △

1 △

2 ▽

4

▷

5 ▽

Saint-Aignan

Chenonceau is a striking example of how the landscape along the Cher, with its charming woods and vineyards, challenged the Loire for the favors of the nobility. However, some more discreet châteaux, such as Saint-Aignan, add their own luster to the river's beauty. The medieval castle of this small fortified town, with its remarkable church and Gothic houses, was demolished to make way for a graceful Renaissance dwelling which looks down over the houses surrounding it. A majestic staircase leads into the courtyard surrounded on two adjacent sides by the buildings of the château, where the octagonal tower of the ceremonial staircase stands proudly. The lantern at its pinnacle is echoed by the sculpted gables of the skylights.

At Saint-Aignan the château, located opposite the church, looks down over the Cher and the small town (1). The formal courtyard and the terraces (2).

Valençay

Although Valençay belongs geographically to the Berry district, its prestigious château cannot be dissociated from the Loire Valley, whether one considers it from the architectural or the historical point of view. A rather plain feudal castle originally stood on the site; but when in 1540 the owner, Jacques d'Estampes, married the daughter of a rich financier, things worked well for both of them, with social standing for the wife and a new château for the husband. The fact that Valençay was thus born under the auspices of High Finance left its mark there for many years to come, as its later owners included a number of Farmers-General, as well as the notorious John Law, whose speculative brand of finance brought on such ruinous inflation. The château's golden age came later, when it became the property of Talleyrand; indeed, that same "lame devil", as he was called, caused Valençay to be chosen in 1808 as the gilded prison in which the princes of Spain, having been overthrown by the Empire, were ordered to live.

As soon as the 12th-century castle had been demolished, Jacques d'Estampes built a rather fanciful keep whose style already had some of the classical features which are much more apparent in the west wing, with its antique pilasters and mansards or bull's eyes, which was added in the 17th century and renovated thereafter.

The formal courtyard and the buildings of the Château of Valençay, which form a right angle (1). The keep (2).

Selles

The curious Château of Selles, which lies hidden among the trees along the banks of the Cher, has several different faces: its rectangular moats, crossed by four bridges, betray the existence of an older fortress, surviving in the form of the Golden Pavilion. Notwithstanding the thickness of the walls, Philippe de Béthune, brother of Sully, built a gracious residence, in the style of the Italian Renaissance, which has lost none of its decorative beauty. However, this setting, despite its charm, was too far removed from the spirit of the age, and Philippe de Béthune decided to build a new residence in order to frame the opposite bridge. These pavilions of red brick and white stone, joined by a long wall above the emblazoned gateway, in the style of a covered way, express the whole of the 17th century. Here, where visitors can see a number of rooms, including the bedroom of the queen of Poland, majesty has taken the place of Italian grace.

The Château of Selles-sur-Cher. The coat-of-arms of Pierre-Philippe de Béthune (1), the porch at the entrance (3), which passes through a long wall leading to two 17th-century buildings (2). The towers of the outer wall are connected by a bridge (4), across the moat. The château seen from the Cher (5).

1 △

2 ▽

5 ▷

3 ◁

4 ▷

Montpoupon

In the Middle Ages Montpoupon was an important defensive position between the Indre and the Cher rivers, or between the châteaux of Loches and Montrichard. The towers from the fortress of that period are still standing, but the residence dates from the 15th century, while the Renaissance turrets of the main gateway are strongly reminiscent of Chenonceau. Although Montpoupon has its own historical associations, we are impressed here by some of the more down-to-earth manifestations of the life of that period. The kitchens, for example, with their monumental array of copper utensils, the delicate clothes in the linen room, the hunting museum, the stables and their outhouses — all suggest that the colorful scene of bygone centuries is about to burst into life again at any minute.

Montrésor

Foulques Nerra, the most brutal of the counts of Anjou, owned a castle at Montrésor, along with nineteen others. The stout defensive walls and the ruined towers of the Late Middle Ages are still imposing, side by side with the gracious residence built in the 15th century by Imbert de Bastarnay, counselor of Louis XI. The château then passed into the hands of the houses of Joyeuse, Brantôme and Beauvilliers, before being acquired by a Polish aristocrat, a companion of Napoleon III.

One of the towers (1) and the residential part (3) of the Château of Montpoupon. At Montrésor, the ruins of the older fortress (2) and the 16th-century château which stands facing it (4).

3 ▷

Loches

The keep at Loches, an enormous rectangular mass with semi-cylindrical counterforts, the finest military structure for which Foulques Nerra took the initiative, was one of the most formidable of its kind in the kingdom. However, while Loches was the setting for the defense of England by the Plantagenets, the southerly defenses of the fortified town had to be constantly reinforced. Indeed, besides the Martelet and the Round Tower, the samples of military engineering which surround the keep — a true encyclopedia of the art of fortifications over the centuries — include features such as the postern and the defensive wall known as the chemise. When the progress of artillery eventually made such things obsolete, the fortress was turned, with equal creativity, into the most dreaded of the State prisons; Ludovico Sforza, as well as the bishops of Autun and Puy languished in its underground dungeon, the Salle de la Question, over the vaulted room in which Cardinal la Balue spent more than ten years experiencing at first hand the cruel "maiden" — a narrow iron cage hanging from the ceiling — which he himself is said to have invented!

After the Royal Gate, at the other end of the ramparts, which formed a genuine entrenched camp around the medieval city and its astonishing collegiate church, with its pyramidal roofs, we come to the royal dwellings, which have many noteworthy historical associations. The Old Dwelling, with its distinctly medieval turrets and indented gables, shows that about the time when Joan of Arc went there to implore Charles VII to go to Reims to be crowned, military matters were always a prime consideration. After he had become sovereign, Charles VII returned to Loches together with the first of the official favorites, Agnes Sorel.

As owner of a château at Beauté, near Paris, she was known as the Lady of Beauty. Agnes Sorel, who during her brief life was the very soul of the château, still haunts Loche to this day, as her tomb, with its remarkable reclining statue of alabaster, never seems to have been left in peace for very long. After difficult negotiations with the canons, it was placed in the collegiate church after her death, then desecrated at the Revolution and later restored in Paris; it was transferred to the Agnes Sorel Tower at Loches, and then to the New Dwelling, which is an

The façade of the Château of Loches (1). The château, opposite the church of St. Ours (2). The covered way on the ramparts (3). The keep, the round tower and the royal dwelling (4).

1 △   2 ▽   4 ▷

3
▷

1 △   2 ▽   3 △

extension of the old. This gracious residence, built during the reigns of Charles VIII and Louis XII, at long last broke away from the art of war, and showed the gentle face of the Renaissance, particularly in the delicate oratory of Anne of Brittany.

The room in the Old Dwelling of the Château of Loches where the records of the trial of Joan of Arc, as well as a 16th-century tapestry, entitled *Musica,* are on display (1). Another room (2). In the Round Tower, the chamber known as the "Question" (3). The dungeon occupied by Ludovico Sforza, who was imprisoned by Louis XII in the Martelet (4). The keep (5). Another statue at the entrance to the Dwelling (6).

Chenonceau

When history and the sure feminine touch happen to come together, an ancient castle looking rather like a mill can be turned into a prodigious vessel of stone, anchored on the Cher. However, before the Château of Chenonceau, which is a universal symbol of all the Loire châteaux, could be built, it was first necessary to remove all traces of a warlike past which had distinctly gone out of fashion. Having evicted the lords of the manor in 1512, Thomas Bohier, Collector of Taxes under three French sovereigns, left nothing of their fortress standing, except the circular keep which is to be seen on the terrace, and even that was heavily renovated. His wife, Catherine Brissonet, then supervised the construction of the dwelling, which is characteristic of the early Renaissance, blending a Gothic structure with an exceedingly Italian ornamentation. However, her efforts were of scant benefit to her and her husband, or even their heirs, since the French Crown confiscated Chenonceau in order to offset the financial irregularities which Bohier had been committing.

On coming to power in 1547, Henri II presented the château to Diane de Poitiers, who was responsible for the majestic garden upstream and the idea of a bridge over the Cher. When dispossessed by her rival Catherine de Médicis, she left the banks of the Cher, a sad and embittered woman, and the Regent then completed her work by laying out a vast park, a new garden, and in particular the gallery on the bridge, which has made Chenonceau a truly unique piece of architecture.

Above the waters of the Cher, the classical sobriety of the plans of Philibert Delorme are

2 △

admirably harmonized with the first dwelling; Cahterine de Médicis was in her element, entertaining frequently and on a grand scale, and allowing her lavish nature to indulge in the worst extravagance, in the style of "Italian" triumphs, though she did not equal the decadence of Rome. A succession of crowned heads came to Chenonceau, including François II, Mary Stuart, Charles IX and Henri III. Henri's young widow was the disconsolate White Lady who had the château draped in

black velvet. After being abandoned for a while, Chenonceau recovered its splendor with George Sand's grandmother, Madame Dupin, at whose brilliant salons Jean-Jacques Rousseau sparkled.

The two-storey gallery of the Château of Chenonceau, above the Cher (1) and the adjacent dwelling (2). The keep and the gardens of Diane de Poitiers (3).

◁ 1

3 ▽

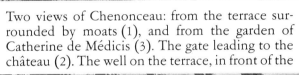

Two views of Chenonceau: from the terrace surrounded by moats (1), and from the garden of Catherine de Médicis (3). The gate leading to the château (2). The well on the terrace, in front of the Tour des Marques (4). The building of the Chancellerie (5). The bedroom of César de Vendôme (6).

5
▷

6
▷

1 △

2 ◁

3 ▽

6
▷

Chenonceau. The Five Queens' Bedroom (1), and the Green Study of Catherine de Médicis, on the ground floor of the gallery (2). The bedroom of Gabrielle d'Estrées (4), on the first floor. Two of the galleries in which tapestries of the 16th and 17th centuries are on display (5 and 8). Here we once again find the salamander, the emblem of François I (3), the numeral signifying Henri II and Catherine de Médicis (6), with the heraldic device of Thomas Bohier, builder of Chenonceau (7). *Following pages:* the château seen in its superb surroundings, on the Cher.

7
▷

4 ▽   5 △

8
▷

Amboise

The plateau on which the Château of Amboise stands looks down over the Île d'Or, one of the oldest passages on the Loire; that does not, however, fully account for its considerable size. Amboise, which had been fortified since time immemorial, managed to escape the control of its counts, who had been ousted by Charles VII, who merely repaired the walls. His son Louis XI chose Amboise as the place of residence for the queen, whose house was unfortunately destroyed during the last century.

Amboise became the gem of French royalty when the Dauphin became Charles VIII. Construction started in 1492 and made rapid progress: at night work proceeded by the light of torches, and in winter the blocks of stone were heated, in order for the mortar to set properly! However, when the king went off to the wars in Italy, and discovered there the kinds of refinement he had dreamt of, he began to regret having acted so hastily. Returning with a star-studded company of craftsmen and artists, as well as an enormous amount of booty, he introduced Italian influence into France, where it marked the end of the Middle Ages. With Fra Giocondo and Il Boccador, the royal abode was filled with riches, while Pacello, the most famous gardener in Italy, laid out the flower beds.

Anne of Brittany inspired a brilliant courtly life; but all of a sudden everything went awry, as a result of a low door lintel, against which the king hit his head, despite his short build, and died a short time later. Anne of Brittany was compelled to marry his successor, Louis XII, whom she followed to Blois.

The Château of Amboise, overlooking the town and the Loire (1 and 5). The Renaissance wing (2 and 3). Detail of the roof of the Gothic wing of the King's Dwelling (4). *Following pages:* the Guard Room and the fireplace of the Cordelières.

1 △

2 △

3 ▽

4 △

5 ▽

The château was briefly eclipsed; but thereafter the new king set about the unhurried construction of a new wing; François I, who had spent his childhood at Amboise, completed it, and the three years which the young king spent there after his accession to the throne were the château's golden age.

Italian influence soared to new heights with the arrival of Leonardo da Vinci; and the festivities, alternating with animal fights, surpassed anything ever seen before. François I, whose refined wit was certainly matched by his valor as a duellist, distinguished himself by nailing to the ground, with his sword, a rampaging wild boar which had been causing panic along the galleries into which it had escaped. At that time the buildings of the château covered the whole of the plateau, thus forming a splendid background for the royal entertainments; both riders and carriages could reach the château without having to dismount, thanks to the spiral ramps which were located inside two enormous towers, Hurault and Les Minimes. Emperor Charles V, on his way to visit François, was left with very unpleasant memories of the Tour des Minimes, because a guard's torch set fire to the tapestries which lined its interior, and he almost suffocated as a result.

From 1527 onwards, the king neglected Amboise, favoring the Paris region instead; the court was then only rarely present at the château. Under François II merrymaking gave way to tragedy, when the Amboise Conspiracy was crushed. He ordered the brutal execution of the Reformers, whose plotting had been divulged; and in the presence of Mary Stuart, his young wife, and Catherine de Médicis, his mother, he then witnessed the atrocities in person. The memory of

Amboise. The sculpted lintel of the doorway of the Saint-Hubert chapel (1). Tapestries by Audenarde (2 and 3). The bedroom of Catherine de Médicis (4). Plaque in the chapel in memory of Leonardo da Vinci (5).

Amboise. The interior of the Saint-Hubert chapel, where Leonardo lies buried (1). The entrance (2) and the Gothic spire (3). *Following pages:* the château buildings and the terrace.

those gentlemen of Brittany, who had died for a cause which the Treaty of Amboise later seemed to recognize, still lingers at the Conspirators' Balcony. Then came the château's decline. Amboise became the property of Gaston d'Orleans, an inveterate

conspirator himself, who eventually saw his fortifications razed to the ground by the royal troops. Once they had reverted to the Crown, the buildings were used as a prison, and then the Empire, which could not afford to maintain them, had many of them demolished. The parts that remain are the most valuable: the royal dwelling and the St. Hubert Chapel, the queen's oratory, where Leonardo da Vinci lies buried. These delicate structures were restored with the greatest care after the bombing of the Second World War, which could well have proved fatal to Amboise.

1 △

2 ▽

Clos-Lucé

Leonardo da Vinci spent the last four years of his life about a quarter of a mile from the château of his royal friend, François I, in the charming manor of Clos-Lucé, which had previously been occupied by Marguerite de Navarre, the sovereign's beloved sister. Leonardo died, in the presence of the king, in one of the bedrooms on the second floor; towards the end of his life he felt he had come to know the "Divine Operator of so many wonderful things", though one is tempted to apply that same expression to himself, when one visits the exhibit, in the basement of the château, of models of some of the ingenious machines he devised.

The manor of Clos-Lucé and its gardens (1 and 2). The bedroom of Leonardo da Vinci (3) and the period kitchens (4).

Plessis-lès-Tours

The château of Plessis-lès-Tours, a plain and unimposing brick building, only remotely brings to mind the residence at which Louis XI stayed so often. But the room where he died, in 1483, still has the distinctive wood paneling in use at the time. Visitors can also see, while at the château, a Museum of Tours Silks — a reminder of the fact that the king moved part of the Lyons silkworks to Tours.

The Château of Luynes (1) and its feudal façade (3). Plessis-lès-Tours (2) and the bedroom in which Louis XI died (4).

1 △

2 ▽

Luynes

Further to the west of Tours, among the vineyards, the Château of Luynes stands on the site of an ancient fortified town, whose aqueduct is still partially visible. Under the name of Maillé this 13th-century castle was the first barony of Touraine; in the 17th century it became a duchy, when the Constable of Luynes acquired it and gave it his name. Throughout the centuries, this plain feudal castle, its round towers embellished by numerous windows, has always been a faithful protector of the region, never leaving the Luynes family.

Villandry

Jean le Breton, Secretary of State of François I, started the construction of Villandry in 1532. It is the last of the great Renaissance châteaux along the banks of the Loire, and marks an interesting phase in the development of architectural thinking. The château does, however, retain some earlier buildings, the 14th-century keep and the external façade of the rear wing. The courtyard, surrounded by buildings on three sides, looks out over the valley formed by the Cher and the Loire, and displays the charms of its period, which include arcaded galleries and mullioned skylights. The decorative details of these features anticipate the style of the classical period.

Yet Villandry owes its fame to another type of architecture, that of its gardens, which are the only ones of their kind in which function and beauty are associated on such a scale. Since 1906 the superb layout devised by the Italian gardeners of the 16th century, complete with a network of canals, fountains and water jets, has been marvelously restored, taking the place of a rather incongruous park in the English style. Here we are in a world made of water, leaves and flowers, rather than of stone and slate.

The gardens, separated by cloisters of greenery, are laid out on three levels: the highest is the water garden, with a vast pond, ringed by promenades lined with linden trees; behind the château the French style is triumphant, in the ornamental garden containing hearts shaped from box and yew

Villandry. View of the château (1). The main courtyard (2). The terraced gardens (3).

1 △

2 ▽

3
▷

1 △

2 ▽

3 ▽

4 △

trees. The more functional aspect of the garden is illustrated by arbors, vine galleries and espalier trees, and spectacularly highlighted in the vegetable garden, a short distance further on. The geometrically shaped beds, with their boxwood borders use the most ordinary vegetables to form an aristocratic decor. Near the old church of Villandry, the flowerbeds consist of medicinal plants, whereas an orchard laid out according to the plans of Androuet du Cerceau, the "Renaissance crown of fruit", is situated on the hillside overlooking the château grounds.

Villandry. The vegetable garden (1 and 4) and the square keep (2). The ornamental garden (3). Inside the château, the picture gallery (5) and the dining room (6).

5 △   6 ▽

Azay-Le-Rideau

Azay-Le-Rideau, which was much admired by the novelist Honoré de Balzac, is truly one of those châteaux which are said to be "feminine". Though of only modest dimensions, and on a much smaller site than Chenonceaux, to which it bears a family resemblance it has immense grace and charm, like the young woman who oversaw its construction, between 1518 and 1529.

Just like Catherine Briçonnet at Chenonceau,

Philippa Lesbahy was the wife of a royal financier, Gilles Berthelot, who was himself too busy to take charge of the construction of the new château. She was therefore responsible for the design of this dwelling which uses the warlike trappings of the Middle Ages, but only for decorative purposes. The

The Château of Azay-le-Rideau (1) and its broad moats (2 and 3).

openings in the walls are now wide windows, rather than loopholes, the battlements have no discernible military function and the moats are placid ponds, in which moldings inspired by those of Blois are reflected. The living quarters inside show an even clearer break with the past; they are large and airy, with sweeping views of a delightful landscape of water and vegetation, and were obviously designed with comfort and pleasure in mind. Instead of an awkward spiral stairs, here we have a grand staircase whose flights are straight; this spectacular structure stands beneath a coffered surbased vault; at the juncture of the ribs, one's eye is drawn by graceful keys with pendants to the medallions which adorn each caisson. Themes cherished by Renaissance Italy — shells, vases, cupids, horns of plenty, griffons and satyrs — adorn the foliage which unfolds steadily throughout the frieze which runs along the steps.

There is another way in which Azay-Le-Rideau parallels Chenonceau. The king, who had just had Semblançay hanged, scrutinized the accounts of his other financiers: the Bohiers were compelled to give their château to their sovereign, while the Berthelot chose instead to flee into exile, where they eventually died. The subsequent history of

Azay-Le-Rideau is somewhat sparse, except for an episode in the war of 1870. Prince Frederick Charles of Prussia, commander of the German army, was banqueting in the grand dining room when the chandelier came crashing down onto the table at which he was seated. Quite sure that an attempt was being made on his life, the prince ordered hostages taken in the village; and it was only with great difficulty that he was dissuaded from having them shot.

Azay-le-Rideau. The large gable of the dwelling (1) in which the grand staircase (3) is located. The Yellow Bedroom (2) and the bed of Pierre de Filley de la Barre (4).

Langeais

Amongst a host of other places, the ruthless "Black Falcon", Foulques Nerra, left his imprint on Langeais: in 944 he built a square keep, now in ruins, on a mound previously occupied by the Carolingians. It is thought to be the oldest in France. At the other end of the spur which overlooks the small town stands the castle of Louis XI, with its equally warlike exterior. Between them, however, is a pleasant garden; a rather austere-looking manor house is situated behind the fortress itself. Despite its somewhat forbidding appearance, the château of Langeais is extremely interesting, as its construction, which started in 1465, was completed in a mere four years; moreover, it was never subsequently remodeled. It is completely furnished and decorated in the style of the period, and thas provides a uniquely vivid picture of the life and times of the lords of the 15th century and of their entourage.

Fearing that the Dukes of Brittany might send further expeditions up the Loire Valley against the French Crown, Louis XI instructed his counsellor Jean Bourré to build new fortifications for an old strategic point, Langeais, which had already seen a great deal of fighting during the period when the Counts of Anjou held it on behalf of the English crown. The problem was not resolved until twenty years later, by diplomatic means, as it were, because

The fortified entrance, with drawbridge (1), of the Château of Langeais (2).

Charles VIII, the son of Louis XI, married Anne of Brittany; and the wedding took place precisely at Langeais.

Though slightly hemmed in by the town's rooftops, the powerful mass of grey stone looks exactly like everyone's image of what a fortress should be: the massive keep was also used as a barracks; deep ditches, now a street, used to yawn in front of the drawbridge; the dwelling-house itself is buttressed by stoutly built towers, while a covered way with machicolations runs all the way around the top of the building. On the courtyard side the military trappings have disappeared, but are not replaced by any ornamentation; indeed the severity of that purely civilian façade, with its dark stonework, reminds one more of Brittany than of the Loire Valley. That must have been to the liking of Louis XI, a man of simple tastes who tended to neglect Amboise (and the queen) for his manor of Plessis-lès-Tours. On a walk through the apartments, the visitor will find some admirable Flemish tapestries and furniture of almost religious solemnity, which illustrate the life style of the Touraine region in the 15th century.

Langeais. The ruins of the keep built by Foulques Nerra (1), opposite the château (2). The Blue Bedroom (3).

78

1 △ 2 ▽ 3 ▽

Langeais. One of the bedrooms contains one of the first four-poster beds (1). Tapestries of the 15th century (2). A painting by Luini and a chest dating from the Italian Renaissance (3). The "thousand-flower" tapestry in the Blue Bedroom (4). The dining room (5).

Ussé

Looking out over the host of rooftops between the Indre and the foliage of the forest of Chinon, purists occasionally regret that the Château of Ussé was so completely restored in the 18th century. The more romantic-minded, however, are glad, seeing in it, after the writer of fairy-tales Charles Perrault, an ideal setting for *Sleeping Beauty*. In any case, the collegiate chapel with its doorway in the form of a triumphal arch, standing alone in the park near a huge cedar, has a Renaissance style so pure that it will delight even the most demanding of critics.

There has been a succession of fortresses on this commanding site ever since the earliest times. The outer walls which one sees today were built in the 15th century; and despite the whiteness of the stone of which they are made, despite the skylights in the roofs and the broad windows in the towers, their military purpose is still evident. The machicolations are not ornamental, and the covered way could still be used for its original purpose. In the

The Château of Ussé looks down over the Indre (1). Its numerous bell-turrets, rising from the park in which the chapel lies half hidden, stand out over the terraced gardens (2). *Following pages:* the courtyard.

17th century, one of Ussé's many owners, in order to make this rather dull place more stylish, did not hesitate to demolish the north wing, facing the parallel valleys of the Indre and the Loire. By hacking down the curtain walls he turned the dark gloomy inner courtyard into a majestic entrance, surrounded by three sections of the château, each with its own compelling charm: Gothic on the left, Renaissance on the right and classical in the rear between them. At the same time a classical pavilion was added opposite the chapel, to take the place of the wing which had been pulled down.

The history of the Château of Ussé was filled with persons who, though they were valiant cavaliers and gracious ladies, were nonetheless of secondary standing; accordingly, it has left us no anecdotes about the great of this world. Yet the living quarters include the traditional King's Bedroom (18th century), as well as some interesting elements from the previous century — a *trompe-l'oeil* ceiling and a grand staircase; the kitchens are also impressive. The ground-floor gallery is hung with Flemish tapestries whose beauty is comparable to that of the Aubusson depicting the life of Joan of Arc in the chapel.

Ussé. The great gallery on the ground floor is adorned with Flemish tapestries (1). A writing desk (2).

Chinon

In the 11th century, Chinon, which had been a Gallo-Roman *oppidum* before becoming a fortress of the Counts of Blois, fell into the hands of the Counts of Anjou; and as soon as one of these, Henri II Plantagenêt, became King of England, it came to symbolize the clash of two hostile nations. Nowadays, the long and largely ruined walls, besieged by vegetation, which are reflected in the Vienne above the slate roofs of the old town, seem to have collapsed beneath the weight of history.

Henri II, who loved to stay at Chinon, was the builder of the greater part of this triple château, including the Fort St. Georges, which derives its name from a chapel dedicated to the patron saint of England. Though the elongated plateau on which it stands is protected on one side by the river and on the other by ravines, the fortress lacked defenses at either end in those days. After the Château du Coudray in the west, Henri II then built this fort, taking care to isolate each of them from the Château du Milieu (the Middle Castle) by broad moats. In 1189 Fort St. Georges, now dismantled, witnessed the final days of the king's life, and the end of an epoch. His son — known to history as Landless John (Jean Sans Terre) — was dispossessed of all his French domains by Philippe-Auguste.

Chinon belonged to the French crown, which had, however, fallen upon lean times. Charles VII, who took refuge in the château, was merely the "king of Bourges". At that point, in 1429, Joan of Arc intervened. In the royal dwelling of the Château du Milieu it is still possible to see the remains of the room where she recognized the sovereign, who was disguised and hidden among his subjects, before persuading him to continue the struggle against the English. Rabelais was born at

1 △   2 ▽

Chinon a short while later; his childhood in the château coincided with the last few years of high living at the château which, having been abandoned by royalty, eventually yielded, like so many others, to the advances of the covetous Cardinal Richelieu. Even so, ever since the 14th century, the bell known as the Marie Javelle has rung on the hour at the top of the Clock Tower.

The Château of Chinon seen from the Vienne (1), and its northern side (2). The Clock Tower (3). The ruins of the royal dwellings (4). *Following pages:* the château seen from the Fort du Coudray.

Montreuil-Bellay

The companions of Foulques Nerra proved to be quite as warlike as their master: Le Berlay, to whom the Black Falcon ceded his estate at Montreuil (hence the town's name) lost no time in turning it into an impregnable fortress. Since their belligerence was matched only by their vindictiveness, the members of that family, which was to produce in the 16th century the poet Joachim du Bellay, attracted the anger of a number of different quarters. Forced to surrender after a siege lasting over a year, the Berlay family saw their keep razed to the ground by Geoffroy Plantegenet, who was at the time Count of Anjou. However, that did not prevent them, later on, from siding with the English against the King of France. Eventually it was Philippe-Auguste who came to subdue them, dismantling the fortress after a long and difficult siege.

Stripped of its warlike attributes, although the outer wall and its towers still stand, Montreuil-Bellay became, over the next few centuries, the pleasant residence of the lords of Melun-Tancarville, and then of Harcourt; the gardens which cas-

1 △   2 ▽   3 △

The Château of Montreuil-Bellay. Two decorative motifs from the fortified section (1 and 2). The outer walls and the ditches (3). The "new" château (4) and the Canons' Residence, in the "small" château (5).

4 ▽   5 ▽

6 ▷

7 ▷

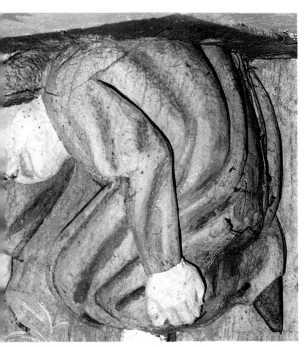

cade down towards the river Thouet are a perfect expression of the château's new purpose. As it is still defended on the town side by a barbican and a moat the only way to gain access is by crossing the bridge and passing through the 13th century gate-house. The castle chapel, which has its was built two centuries later, has its own bridge, a vigorous and elegant structure nicely matching the Château Neuf, which faces it. This New Castle, the pride of Montreuil-Bellay, is a consummate example of ogival art, attached to two round 12th-century towers. The gracious tower overlooking the court-yard, its six windows adorned with delicately carved false balustrades, was made famous by the Duchess of Longueville, who once rode up its grand staircase on horseback! After she had been exiled by Louis XIV, this former participant in the aristocratic rebellion against the crown known as La Fronde, led a lavish life at Montreuil-Bellay, as the château's rich furnishings testify; the visitor is, how-ever, even more likely to be moved by the sound of a motet, the score of which is part of a 15th-century

painting on the ceiling, and which is played during the tour.

The more modest Petit Château, somewhat overwhelmed by its noble neighbor, is nonetheless a highly original miniature. One of its wings contains a kitchen with a central fireplace, its four arcades supporting an octagonal pyramid with an opening at the top to allow the smoke to escape. The other wing, the Dwelling of the Monks, has a most unusual layout: each of its four pepper-pot towers leads to a separate private dwelling, as well as its cellar. One should definitely stroll around the château's splendid Gothic cellars, whose wine press was still in service at the beginning of the century. This was the good life, in Anjou . . .

Montreuil-Bellay. Vaulting adorned with heraldic devices (1). The kitchens, from the Gothic period (2), the dining room (5) and the drawing room (8). The beams are decorated with grotesque figures (3, 4, 6 and 7).

8 ▷

Montsoreau

It is very difficult to dissociate the name of Montsoreau from that of the Famous Lady — in fact, when one takes a closer look at French history, several famous ladies come to mind, the most famous of them, the wife of the elder Alexandre Dumas, being fictitious. But reality turns out to be quite as good as fiction. First of all there was Nicole de Chambes, who seduced the Duke of Berry and helped establish the League for the Public Good, in 1472. At the St. Bartholomew's Day massacre of Protestants, a century later, one of those who took part most fiercely in the killings was the lord of Chambes; he was assassinated, his château, as well as his fiancée being bequeathed to his brother (this was the Françoise de Méridor whom Dumas brought to the stage under the name of Diane). This fickle woman fell in love with Bussy d'Amboise, Governor of Anjou; her husband, having learnt of their relationship, made her arrange to meet him. Bussy fell into the ambush and was killed by a pistol shot; the now reconciled spouses proceeded to spend forty happy years together.

From the Château of Montsoreau there is a superb view of the Loire (1). The house named after La Dame de Montsoreau contains, in its main bedroom (3), a fine 16th-century fireplace (2). The Château of Saumur occupies a dominant position overlooking the valley (4).

1 △

Saumur

Unlike so many other châteaux, Saumur was first a lordly residence, which was only later changed into a fortress – a feature which accounts for its special appeal. Naturally enough, its commanding position, above a sheer drop into the Loire, had long been used for military purposes; indeed no fewer than three buildings – one per century – had preceded the present château, which was built by the Dukes of Anjou in the second half of the 14th century. The miniature of *Les Très Riches Heures du duc de Berry*, in which it is depicted so enticingly, reminds one of princes such as Louis I and Louis II, with their fondness for beautiful things. The pinnacles, weathervanes and other similar ornaments have disappeared from the rooftops, and Saumur did not remain for very long the Château of Love, so celebrated by the good King René, the last of the Dukes of Anjou.

Having become a focal point of the Protestant faith at the end of the 16th century, the town was given by Henri III to the King of Navarre as a safe place. The future King Henri IV then chose as Governor of Saumur the faithful Duplessis-Mornay. This fervent Calvinist, who was both a soldier and a scholar, did more than merely fortify the château with the star-shaped buttresses which can still be seen today; he also founded a theological academy. The town thereupon became a "second Geneva", and even today Saumur has not recovered the standing which it enjoyed at the time. But the Revocation of the Edict of Nantes dealt the town a fatal blow. Serving first as a governor's residence, the château lost all its prestige, being turned into a prison for salt-smugglers; it was here that Fouquet, the Controller of the Royal Finances who had committed the capital blunder of making Louis XIV jealous of his wealth, was imprisoned.

The southwest wing, which contains his dungeon, still looks very much like a prison — inevitably, perhaps, as during the Empire the château continued to perform this most undignified function. Previously the opposite wing had been pulled down to make way for a terrace, from which, despite the disruption of the building's homogeneity, the view is superb. The château was restored in the last century, and the barracks which it formerly housed now consists of two interesting museums, devoted to the decorative arts and the horse. The first of these contains a fine collection of works of art, whereas the other deals thoroughly with the history of the horse, with special emphasis of Saumur as quintessential riding country.

2 ▽

Saumur. The formal courtyard of the château (1), its windows embellished by sculpted balustrades (2). The fortified main entrance (3) and the well hoist system in the central courtyard (5). A Museum of the Decorative Arts is located inside the château (4).

Le Pont de Varenne

Not far to the north of Doué-la-Fontaine, the manor of Le Pont de Varenne stands reflected in the moats, which draw their water from a tributary of the Layon; but the sole reminder of the days when they fulfilled a military function is a solitary round tower. This idyllic dwelling, which has been much tampered with over the centuries, is adorned in particular with a fine early Gothic crozier pediment.

The south façade of the manor of Pont-de-Varenne, which dates from the 15th and 16th centuries (1). The Château of Montgeoffroy (3) and its original period kitchens (2).

Montgeoffroy

Three long tree-lined avenues lead to this exceedingly stylish residence, built in 1772 for the Marshal de Contades. Since then nothing has changed, as Montgeoffroy is still inhabited by the same family. The architect Nicolas Barré made judicious use of the existing 16th-century building, incorporating two of its round towers and the chapel into the wings which are attached to an impressive main residence, which has a fine slate roof and pink brick chimneys. The living quarters are furnished as they were originally, blending good taste with the refinement of works by the greatest names in cabinet-making, painting and tapestry. Moreover, the beautiful stained-glass window in the chapel, depicting the Adoration of the Shepherds and the Three Wise Men, should certainly be seen.

1 △

2 ▽

Brissac

"A new half-built château, in an old half-destroyed château": this is how the present Duke of Brissac describes the imposing residence in which his family has lived for close to half a millenium. And it is truly a huge composite, half-completed structure. In the 15th century, on foundations which can be traced back to Foulques Nerra, Pierre de Brézé built an enormous feudal castle which was bought by the Duke of Brissac, René de Cossé. His grandson Charles, one of the marshals in the family, decided around the year 1600 to erect an ambitious seven-storey dwelling. His death suspended construction at the fourth floor, while the remains of the feudal castle had not yet been demolished — a fact which accounts for the curious arrangement of the thick round towers. In this way, Gothic and early Baroque, fortress and palace came to share the same site, in the midst of a magnificent park.

Since then the Dukes of Brissac have sought to keep alive the spirit of this sumptuous abode. In the château's hundred and fifty rooms, whose ceilings, sculpted and painted in the French style, are matched by august staircases or monumental fireplaces, the furniture is equal to its surroundings. We see, for example, Flemish, Brussels or Gobelins tapestries, chandeliers of Venetian crystal, collections of porcelain and silverware, and also a portrait gallery, which includes a name renowned in the world of champagne, La Veuve Clicquot, who was an ally of the family.

The façade of the Château of Brissac-Quincé, which was rebuilt in the 17th century (1) and the entire château with the Round Tower, its sole surviving medieval feature (2). The chapel (3). One of the bedrooms draped with tapestries; the ceiling decorations are of the 17th century (4). Heraldic devices (5).

3 △

4 ◁

5 ▷

Angers

It seems curious that Angers, the city of gentle living and refinement, should have turned its back on the nearby banks of the Loire, and chosen as a setting for its slate roofs the land on either side of the Maine. After battling both Romans and Normans, Angers asserted its identity at a very early date through the Counts of Anjou, from Foulques the Good in the 10th century up to King René: many of them were fierce warriors, but none of them neglected the things of the mind. Evidence of this is provided by the renowned university they founded in Angers and the support they gave the fine arts.

In 1246 St. Louis elevated Anjou to the status of county-peerage, awarded it as a fief to his young brother Charles, and built for him the brooding fortress with its seventeen towers on a white stone foundation. This was a period of grand, lavish deeds, epitomized by the extraordinary Apoca-

lypse Tapestry. Notwithstanding incessant wars, Duke Louis commissioned Nicolas Bataille to execute this lengthy masterpiece from cartoons by the official painter of Charles V. This monumental work, whose total length is 551 ft., was bequeathed to the cathedral by King René. Having been discarded and eventually used as sackcloth, this oldest surviving French tapestry was recovered in an incomplete state. It is now on display in a room specially built to accomodate it. The fortress was completed by Louis II and King René, who made it a setting for endless festivities. After it became the property of the Crown, Angers went into a decline; Henri III decapitated the towers, which, until the recent restoration, were used as prisons.

Angers. The ramparts of the château and the Tour du Moulin, seen from inside the outer wall (1). The north postern (2). The château seen from the Maine (3) and from the east (4). The towers are made of schist striped with white stone (5).

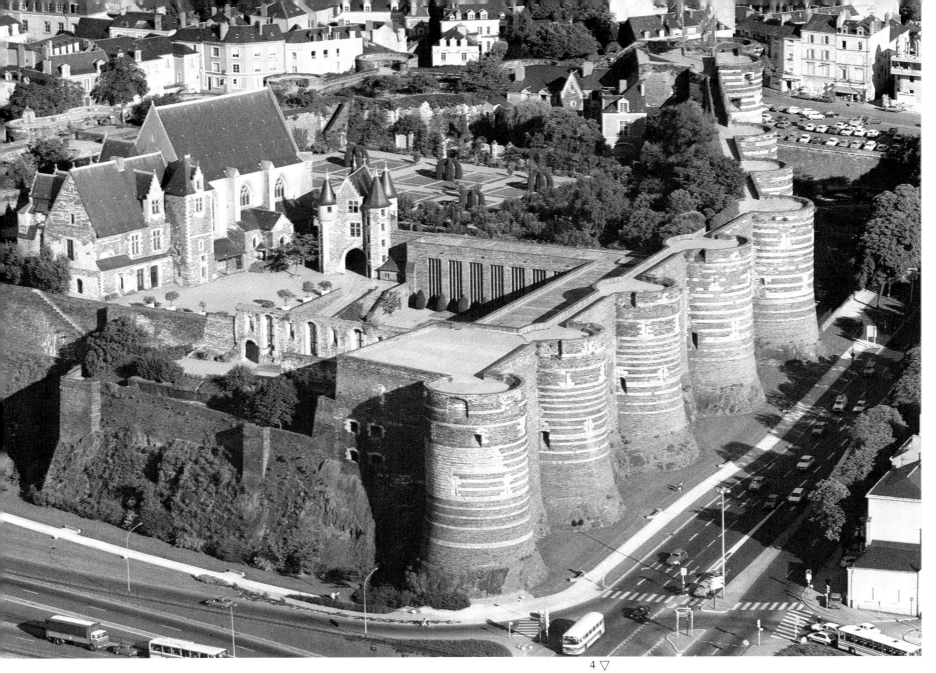

4 ▽

Following pages: Angers. The Governor's Dwelling, inside the outer wall of the château (1). One of the tapestries of the Apocalypse (2). The Royal Dwelling (3).

5
▷

1 △   2 ▽   3 ▷

o hōme quy la pōme priz , La
regarde cy le poure priz , Et
de judas quy par trahyſon ,
par enuie et contre Raiſon , Ar
judas ly fut moult diligent , I
car pour trente deniez dargent ,
helas il en fut grant marche ,
le ſaunēur en fut detrache ,

Serrant

The Château of Serrant, built of brown schist and light tuff above dark moats, has a fine unity of style, which is surprising when one considers that it took more than a century and a half to complete. Construction started in 1546, from plans drawn up by Philibert Delorme (and which were at all times respected), but Serrant was not finished until the building of the chapel, the work of Hardouin-Mansart in 1705, and the mausoleum sculpted by Coysevox for the Marquis of Vaubrun. The château's inner courtyard, opposite the round towers, has a monumental 17th-century gateway; the romantic park, with its broad expanse of water, is much more recent.

The upper floor, whose coffered ceilings match the grandeur of the majestic staircase, were home to Louis XIV and Napoleon I, including other notable guests. The interior of Serrant is a veritable feast of refinement, wherever one looks: lavishly appointed state rooms, a rich library, Flemish and Brussels tapestries, a superb Italian study, portraits by the masters and a bust of Empress Marie-Louise by Canova.

Serrant. The three buildings which make up the château (1). An Italian ebony cabinet of the 17th century (2), the great staircase (3) and the portal (4). The east façade (5). *Following pages:* the inner courtyard.

2

Le Plessis-Bourré

Jean Bourré, in 1468, was a happy man: Secretary of Finance under Louis XI and Treasurer of France, he had just been engaged in the construction of the Château of Langeais on behalf of his sovereign; now, he was about to build, from the ground up, and for himself, an ideal residence on the estate of Plessis-le-Vent. He had enormous moats dug out and, in the middle of them, he built a square dwelling flanked by three towers and a keep. Five years later, Le Plessis-Bourré was finished; it was, at the time, one of the most beautiful châteaux in France.

Thick walls, a platform for artillery, a gatehouse and a 140-ft. bridge across the moats, ending in a drawbridge, all certainly add up to a fortress. Yet within this rugged setting there is a jewel that even visiting monarchs were going to envy — among them Louis XI, of course, and also Charles VIII, François I and Henri IV. The St. Anne chapel, the Hall of Justice, the guardroom, with the vivid racy paintings which cover its wooden ceilings; the library and the reception rooms all transport the visitor into the life and times of a French lord of the late 15th century.

The Château of Le Plessis-Bourré, its moats and its 140-ft. long bridge (1 and 3). The Guard Room and its famous painted wood coffered ceiling (15th century) (2).

1

Le Lude

On the borders of Touraine, Maine and Anjou the Château of Le Lude stands reflected in the waters of the Loir. Its majestic Louis XVI pediment is flanked on the north by a 16th-century façade and, on the south, by a wing whose style is a mixture of Louis XII and François I. The courtyard thus formed to the rear is closed by an 18th-century portico. The château is therefore very much a composite work. Yet it has a certain harmonious integrity about it; nowadays, moreover, it is famous for its sound and light shows.

The Château of Le Lude and the Loir River (1).

Other Châteaux of the Loire valley

Beaugency

On account of the importance it had until modern times as a site commanding the only bridge over the Loire between Blois and Orléans, Beaugency was fought over repeatedly throughout the centuries — a fact illustrated by the tattered state of its fortifications. What now remains is the Devil's Tower, built in the 12th century, and the keep, which is even older, as can be seen from its rectangular design and massive buttresses.

Chateauneuf

The "New Castle" after which the town is named was built in the Middle Ages, and disappeared long ago. In the 17th century, where it had once stood, the Grand Master of Ceremonies, La Vrillière, erected a miniature Versailles, which was dismantled after the Revolution. All that is left now is the domed rotunda, currently in use as the town hall, in a pleasant park.

Meung-sur-Loire

After serving as a prison for the poet François Villon, and as headquarters for the English, and then for Joan of Arc once she had driven them out, the Château of Meung-sur-Loire dates back to the 12th century, but was later remodeled, particularly in the 18th century.

The keep at Beaugency (1). All that remains of the Château of Châteauneuf-sur-Loire, now a town hall, is its dome (2). The formal entrance to the Château of Meung-sur-Loire (3).

1 △

2 ▽

3 ▷

Beauregard

This former hunting lodge of François I, hidden within a secluded estate at the edge of the Forest of Bussy, was enlarged and embellished when it became the residence of ministers who where also patrons of the arts. At the beginning of the 17th century Paul Ardier, Treasurer of Savings under Louis XIII, added a wing, and in particular the celebrated Gallery of Illustrious Persons, the sole specimen of a type of decoration much favored at the time: the portraits of 363 kings and eminent persons, arranged in bays throughout this long room. The floor of the gallery is covered with Delft tiles depicting a whole army on the march in the time of Louis XIII, complete with cavalry, infantry, artillery and musketeers.

Fougères-sur-Bièvre

The Château of Fougères-sur-Bièvre, a short distance from Cheverny, is an old fortress which has retained its square 11th-century keep. The rest of

1 △

2 ◁

3 ▷

4 ▽

the building was erected, starting in 1470, by Pierre Le Refuge, Louis XI's Minister of Finance, who remained faithful to tradition in that the design he chose was that of a defensive castle located on a plain. The covered gallery of the inner courtyard, with its surbased arches resting on octagonal pillars (like the Charles d'Orléans wing at Blois) was the work of his son-in-law. Visitors to the château can see the admirably harmonious beams, arranged in the shape of a ship's keel, in the principal dwelling.

The Château of Beauregard (1) and its Gallery of Illustrious Persons, which comprises 363 historical portraits (5). At Fougères-sur-Bièvre, the inner courtyard of the château, the square keep, the Dwelling and the look-out turret (2 and 3). The remains of the feudal castle of Lavardin (4).

5 ▷

Lavardin

In the 12th century Lavardin, situated overlooking the Loir, was the seat of the Counts of Vendôme; until 1590, when Henri IV ordered it dismantled, its strategic position had cost it a great number of assaults. The château's romantic ruins still include some interesting Gothic details and enable one to see the triple outer wall which kept invaders, particularly Richard Lionheart, at bay. After the 14th-century gatehouse, an underground corridor leads through the outer wall built in the 15th century and to the chemise wall, which protects the rectangular keep so typical of the 11th century. The staircase inside the keep is still serviceable.

Ménars

The central part of this 17th-century château was acquired by Madame de Pompadour, who commissioned the architect Gabriel to give it the majestic beauty it now has. And with its superb outbuildings and its refined park descending in terraces towards the Loire, Ménars is truly a sumptuous château. The royal favorite did not, however, enjoy it for long, as she died only four years after buying it. Her brother, the Marquis of Marigny, completed the renovation with the help of the architect Soufflot, and made certain alterations in the gardens, which contain a Temple of Love, the Baths of the Marchioness, as well as all the sculpted devices which were so common in this kind of setting in 17th-century France.

Mer

Upstream from Blois, and a short distance from the Loire, there is, in the small town of Mer, a residence from the same period as Ménars, though much more modest in both size and decor.

Montrichard

A mere glance at this square keep overlooking the Cher suggests that it must have been the work of Foulques Nerra. And it certainly was. The unrelenting warrior built it in defiance of the Count of Blois. After being reinforced by a second defensive wall in the 12th century, it received a third one in 1250. However, as the populace had been unwilling to recognize a king who was at the time Protestant, Henri IV had the keep reduced from its "infamous heights" to its present ruined state.

The Château of Chantecaille, at Mer (1). The ruins of Montrichard, of which the square keep is still standing (2). The Château of Ménars, on the bank of the Loire (3).

1 △

2 ◁

3 ▷

1 △

2 △

4 ▷

3 ▽

La Possonnière

The fief of La Possonnière was acquired on his return from Italy by Loys de Ronsard, the father of Pierre de Ronsard, the poet, who was born within these walls in 1524 and spent his childhood here. Since then nothing has changed. The elegant manor built in the Italian style still has numerous carved inscriptions. At the top of the staircase turret, the family coat of arms (azure with three fish argent) proclaims, in Latin, the Ronsard motto: "The future belongs to merit".

Carved Latin inscriptions and Renaissance moldings (1, 2 and 3) adorn the windows of the manor of La Possonnière, in which the poet Ronsard was born. A view of the manor (4). The doors of the outbuildings (5).

5 △

Vendôme

The first Counts of Vendôme fortified a very old defensive site near an island in the Loir, and steadily enriched it. But the Revolution has left little of it standing. Its remains include the thick Poitiers Towers (so named because the count of Poitiers was imprisoned there) and several pieces from the superb mausoleums in which Antoine de Bourbon and Jeanne d'Albret were buried, as well as from the collegiate church of St. Georges.

Troussay

In the last century, this appealing Renaissance manor house was owned by the historian Louis de la Saussaye; the fact that it bears, on its rear façade, the famous sculpted porcupine does not mean that Louis XII resided there. It simply means that the residence was restored and embellished through the efforts of this dedicated man, using decorative components drawn from the ruined buildings of the region.

Villesavin

Jean le Breton, superintendent of construction at Chambord, had the craftsmen and workers of the royal residence build him the Château of Ville-savin. The result, which has come down to us practically intact, is a charming Renaissance dwelling displaying certain classical tendencies. Its beauty is further enhanced by features such as its rare 16th-century dovecote with feet, and an Italian basin of white marble.

The ruins of the Château of Vendôme, overlooking the Loir; only the Poitiers Tower was rebuilt, in the 15th century (1). The Château of Troussay, not far from Cheverny — truly a Renaissance country house (2). At the Château of Villesavin, ornate skylights (3), the salamander, emblem of François I (4), and the bust of that same monarch (5).

2 ▽

3 △

4 ◁

5 ▷

Blancafort

This handsome 15th-century building of pink brick was scarcely remodeled at all when the Faucon family acquired it in the 17th century, the period in which the courtyard, flanked by two pavilions, was laid out. Whereas the park situated on the right bank of the Sauldre has been left in a semi-natural state, the forbidding walls of the château look down over the curved flowerbeds of a garden in the French style. The library of the Château of Blancafort, adorned with Regency wood paneling, is particularly interesting, as is the dining room, which is draped with repoussé and painted Flemish leather and with fine tapestries of the 17th and 18th centuries.

Boucart

In 1560 Franciscus de Bocart, grand master of artillery, affixed his name to the north wing which forms the third side of the courtyard of the Château of Boucart. During the reign of Louis XIV the

Marshal of Navailles remodeled Boucart by adding to the moats a number of stretches of water supplied by the Sauldre, as well as a French garden, which now unfortunately exists no more. In the Renaissance wing, visitors can see handsomely furnished drawing rooms and a kitchen still equipped with a mechanical spit of the period.

La Chapelle d'Angillon

In the 12th century, this "Château de Béthune", which derives its name from the Duke of Sully who became its new owner shortly after 1600, was the fief of the principality of Boisbelle, a small free and tax-exempt state. It has the square layout, the moats, the round towers and the keep which are so characteristic of the Middle Ages, at the edge of a pleasant terrace leading down to a pond. The dwelling received a great deal more light and air in the 16th century, when skylights and mullioned windows were added, and turret staircases were built. "Le Jeu de Paume" is the name given to a gallery

near the well, whose two fine arcades are also evidence of changes inspired by the Renaissance.

La Verrerie

In perfect harmony with its natural environment, La Verrerie was originally the work of Charles VII, who gave it to Jean Stuart, his ally against the English. Construction was completed around 1525; then the family line died out, and the château reverted to the Crown. Louis XIV, however, ceded it to the favorite of Charles II of England, the Duchess of Portsmouth (actually Louise de Kéroualle). And it is thanks to her that the English aristocracy is still present in this Sologne in which Scottish craftsmen, especially glaziers and weavers, have left their imprint.

Façade of the Château of Blancafort (1). Moats surround the Château of Boucard (2). The Château of Béthune, at La Chapelle-d'Angillon (3). la Verrerie, near D'Aubigny-sur-Nère, gracefully situated at the edge of a lake (4).

3 △   4 ▽

1 △

2 ▷

Argy

This square 15th-century keep, with its trefoil machicolations, with flanking watchtowers, is a fine example of military architecture. Remodeled by Charles de Brissac, a companion of Louis XII, Argy displays a rather grim curtain wall which runs between the keep and the seigniorial tower. However, while the message conveyed by its outward appearance is one of military efficiency, on the courtyard side of the château we see a comfortable residence, more French than Italian. The double gallery consisting of florid accolades surmounted by basket-handle arches, the façades adorned with initials and plant motifs, and the colonnettes extending into pinnacles provide a thorough illustration of the skills of Renaissance artists.

3 ▽

Azay-le-Ferron

The façade of the Château of Azay-le-Ferron summarizes four centuries of architectural history, in that the round tower is from the 15th century, the François I pavilion from the 16th, the Humières wing, which links the two, from the 17th, and the Breteuil pavilion from the 18th. Our education is taken a stage further by the park, in which we see the contrast between an English garden and box and yew trees neatly clipped in the French style, and also by the wide range of furniture, spanning the centuries, to be found in the apartments. The Empire and Restoraton styles are most fully represented, though there are also some Renaissance tapestries and a number of large paintings from the school of Genoa (17th century).

Château-Guillaume

The château where Aliénor of Aquitaine is thought to have been born, and which belonged for many years to the La Trémoïlle family, looks down from a commanding position above a picturesque village with roofs of flat tiles, in the valley of the Allemette. The buildings located on this site, whose strategic importance has always been evident, particularly during the Middle Ages, have frequently been altered over the ages.

The machicolated tower of the Château of Azay-le-Ferron (1) and the great living room with its coffered ceiling (2). Château-Guillaume (3) which was extensively renovated in the last century. Argy: the keep (5), the gallery (4) and moldings (6).

4 △

5 ◁

6 ▷

1 △

2
◁

3
▷

La Ferté-Imbault

The son-in-law of Thibault the Trickster, Count of Blois, built a fortress at this spot. Having been destroyed during the Hundred Year's War, it was rebuilt, only to be dismantled once again during the Wars of Religion, and finally re-erected by Jacques d'Étampes, Marshal of France.

Sarzay

This proud feudal abode, with a tiled roof, was used by George Sand as a model for the Château of Blanchemont in *The Miller of Angibault.*

Les Reaux

This manor from the late 15th century, with its fancy gatehouse, was owned by the memorialist Tallemant des Réaux, who is known for his *Short Stories,* in which he painted a picture of society in the 17th century.

The châteaux of La Ferté-Imbault (1) and Sarzay (2). Les Réaux, near Bourgeuil (3). The ruins of Villentrois (4).

Villentrois

The ruins of the feudal castle of Villentrois tower over the village, which lies astride the banks of the Modon, in an area which was once famous for the gun-flints which it produced.

Bridoré

In the 14th century, Jean de Boucicault and his son, both Marshals of France, built the fortress of Bridoré, which was remodeled by Imbert de Bastarnay, the Grand Chamberlain of Louis XI. With its polygonal defense system it was the safest stronghold in the region. The dry moats which run around its towers and fortifications contain some interesting caponiers, or protected passageways with openings through which weapons could protrude from the side of the ditch.

Château-Renault

The small town of Château-Renault, founded in the 11th century by Renault, son of Geoffroy de Château-Gontier, stands on high ground overlooking the confluence of the Brenne and the Gault. There is accordingly a fine view from the terraces of the château, which are shaded by linden trees. A 14th-century gate, surmounted by hoardings, leads onto the terraces.

Chanteloup

The Duke of Choiseul, exiled to his estate near Amboise by Louis XV, turned away from cares of state to busy himself with the fine arts; he surrounded himself with an intellectual and artistic court which sustained a miniature Versailles all of its own. The duke wanted an original building to testify to the fidelity of his friends; and, as oriental art was very much in fashion at the time, he commissioned his architect, Camus de Mézières, to build the pagoda which is all that now remains of the château.

Le Coudray-Montpensier

In this region which Rabelais used as the setting for the Picrocholine War in his *Gargantua* (the manor of La Devinière, where he spent much of his childhood is nearby), the Château of La Coudray-Montpensier was completed in 1481 by Louis I of Bourbon-Montpensier.

Bridoré (1). Château-Renault (2). South of Amboise (3).

Cinq-Mars-La-Pile

This village, whose curious name derives from a structure of unknown origin, contains the remains of the château of the man who was the favorite of Louis XIII. Cinq-Mars quarreled with Richelieu, tried to have him assassinated, was discovered and died on the scaffold at the age of twenty-two. The cardinal, as could have been expected from a man with so much experience in this particular field, had his enemy's château destroyed.

Genillé

The graceful manor of Genillé, built towards the end of the 15th century, and noted for a remarkable dovecote, blends harmoniously with the village which stretches out below it towards the banks of the Indrois.

The Château of Coudray-Montpensier (1), not far from Chinon. The two towers of Cinq-Mars-la-Pile (2). The Château of Genillé (3).

129

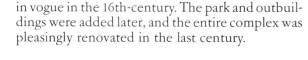

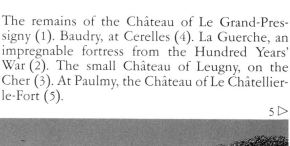

Le Grand-Pressigny

This château, which is now a museum of prehistory, has a number of very interesting architectural remains. It is one of the earliest Romanesque keeps in the Loire Valley; machicolations were added to it in the 15th century, and it was also attached to the octagonal Vironne Tower, which is surmounted by a balustrade and a dome. In the middle of the 16th century the château was remodeled by the marquis of Villars, who was responsible for the covered arcaded gallery.

La Guerche

Its foundations level with the waters of the Creuse, La Guerche used to defend the passage along the river, which is crossed at this point by a Roman road. The château, which was built around 1450 by André Villequier, the Grand Chamberlain of Charles VII, is most notable for its two basements. Stores, a prison and a granary (the grain chutes can still be seen in the walls) were once housed beneath its vaulted ceilings.

Leugny

In the 18th century André Portier, a pupil of the architect Jacques III Gabriel, performed this stylistic exercise on an estate which had belonged to the Descartes family: he covered his château with slate, placed a stone balustrade on top and adorned the windows of the upstairs floor with consoles. The equally harmonious interior decor, with its elegant moldings and noble fireplaces, is enhanced by its Louis XVI furniture.

Baudry

Just north of Tours, on the site of a former feudal castle, Baudry displays the pavilions and the brick towers with light-colored ties which were so much in vogue in the 16th-century. The park and outbuildings were added later, and the entire complex was pleasingly renovated in the last century.

Paulmy

The D'Argenson family, which had long been established in Touraine, produced some distinguished statesmen. One of them, the marquis of Paulmy, though in fact Minister of War, spent all his time working on history, buried within the most abundant library of his day.

The remains of the Château of Le Grand-Pressigny (1). Baudry, at Cerelles (4). La Guerche, an impregnable fortress from the Hundred Years' War (2). The small Château of Leugny, on the Cher (3). At Paulmy, the Château of Le Châtellier-le-Fort (5).

1 △

La Roche-Racan

Jacques Gabriel, the first of a dynasty of famous architects, built the château in 1634 for Honorat de Bueil, marquis of Racan. This nobleman would have wished to be known to posterity for his feats of arms, but this proved beyond his reach; he was equally unsuccessful in his love for Sylvie, Chloris and Arténice; however, as a founder-member of the French Academy, and a pastoral poet who lamented these lost loves in his *Stanzas on Retirement,* this disciple and friend of the poet Malherbe, who withdrew for forty years into this bucolic setting, did leave an imprint of sorts on history.

Le Rivau

The romantic Château of Rivau, highlighted by the open parkland surrounding it, is mentioned in the stories of Rabelais as a gift from Gargantua to one of the knights in the war of King Picrochole. And it certainly still has a very special atmosphere. It was a 13th-century stronghold fortified by Pierre de Beauvau, Chamberlain of Charles V, and also distinguished itself before the siege of Orléans, when its stables made it possible for Joan of Arc to upgrade the equipment of her force. The keep adjoins a dwelling which is flanked by two towers, one for the chapel and the other for a handsome polygonal staircase. Nowadays the apartments, whose decor includes both Gothic and Renaissance, are used for exhibitions.

Montbazon

The quadrangular keep at Montbazon is one of the colossal landmarks which Foulques Nerra built across his county in order to assert himself against the Counts of Blois, his perennial rivals. The religious statue located above the two surviving floors of the château therefore has as its base the deeds of the Black Falcon. Yet it is not as incongruous as it may seem, for this terrifying warrior periodically inflicted upon himself the worst penance in order to atone for his sins; indeed he took up his pilgrim's staff, without hesitation, on three separate occasions, and set off for Jerusalem!

The Romanesque keep of Montbazon, with its statue of the Virgin (1). La Roche-Racan (2). In the castle of Le Riveau (3), the King's Bedroom (4) and the Renaissance four-poster bed in the bedroom of the Oratory (5).

2 ▽

3 △

4
◁

5
▷

Saché

This plain 16th-century manor, which was remodeled in the 18th, was made famous by the novelist Honoré de Balzac, who stayed there a number of times. In the last century the property belonged to one of his friends, M. de Margonne, and the author of *The Human Comedy* loved to take refuge at Saché, to escape both the commotion of Paris and the clutches of his creditors. His memory is preserved in a small museum, and his bedroom remains now as it was then, the bed in the alcove, the desk and the armchair. Balzac once wrote of Saché: "My view from there encompasses the Indre and the little château which I have decided to call the 'Gourd-Bell'. The silence is wonderful." While at Saché

Balzac wrote a number of works, including *Father Goriot, The Quest for the Absolute* and part of *The Lily in the Valley,* which takes place on the banks of the Indre. There are a number of rooms devoted to portraits, manuscripts, original editions and assorted memorabilia from the period.

Saché, where Balzac once stayed (1 and 3). The novelist's bedroom (2) has been kept just as it was during his lifetime.

Tours

The city of Tours has no château of its own commensurate with its history. On the banks of the Loire one has to be content with the Tour de Guise (11th century), from which the son of Scarface escaped after his father's assassination. It is situated not far from the Pavillon de Mars, which was built during the reign of Louis XVI.

Vaujours

Nestling amongst an untamed landscape, the castle known in the Middle Ages as Val Joyeux (now the name of a nearby lake) still looks distinctly melancholy today. Brambles have crept all over its dilapidated towers and walls; and where the river once flowed and filled the moats there is now nothing but swamp. A barbican stands in front of the outer defensive wall, with its curiously embossed round towers, one of which still has its machicolations. The remains of the chapel and the 15th-century seigniorial dwelling can still be seen in the courtyard.

These moving ruins which turn pink in the sun bring to mind the famous Louise de la Bame le Blanc, of Touraine, who became lady-in-waiting to Madame, the king's sister-in-law, before conquering the royal heart. However, the woman who was to become the Duchess of La Vallière and Vaujours came only once within these walls, in 1669. At that time she was no longer the favorite of the Sun King, having been ousted by Madame de Montespan, and was to retire to a convent.

Tours. The Château and the Tour de Guise (1). The ruins of the fortified castle of Vaujours (2).

1 △

2
▷

Baugé

At Baugé it is known as the Château of King René. In fact Good King René, in 1455, did supervise the construction of this appealing abode. This disarmingly casual sovereign, who hated solemnity, may indeed have advised his masons to carve their own images on the rear watchtower. In any case, like his mother Yolande of Aragon, who had defeated the English at the city gates, he was happy at Baugé, spending his time painting and writing verse, or hunting wild boar in the Forest of Chandelais.

Boumois

Behind this early-16th-century château, a perfect feudal fortress of the type found in flat terrain, there is a seigniorial dwelling of essentially Gothic design, but with Renaissance decor. On the staircase leading to it the visitor will see an admirable wrought-iron lock bearing the coat of arms of René de Thory, the lord of the manor and a slightly sinister figure: in 1529 this haughty gentleman married the beautiful Anne d'Asse, a sort of embodiment of Diana the huntress, after each of them had disposed permanently of their respective spouses.

1 ◁

2 ▽

Challain-La-Potherie

Challain-la-Potherie, located on the banks of the Argos, which forms a small lake at this point, is actually close to the border of Brittany; its château, however, does not belong to that province, as it is a magnificent neo-Gothic structure — a difficult exercise which the 19th century did not hesitate to undertake. This noble dwelling was the property of the La Rochefoucauld family.

Les Briottières

The Château des Briottières, set among tall trees, next to a small lake, in the heart of a 200-acre-park, is a magnificent 18th-century residence, for which the Baroque is not synonymous with extravagance.

Baugé (1). The outer façade of the Château of Boumois (2). At Challain-la-Potherie, the 19th-century château known as "the Chambord of Anjou" (3). Another 19th-century château, in a more sober style — Les Brottières, at Champigné (4).

1 △   2 ▽   3 ▷

Chanzeaux

The Château of Chanzeaux is situated on the heights of Le Layon, in the midst of a cluster of vine-growing villages. The 19th-century structure, before which there are some very large outbuildings, is a fine example of a neo-Gothic deeply imbued with romanticism.

Champtoceaux

Perched on the top of a wooded hill near the edge of the Nantes region, Champtoceaux was a prize over which the Counts of Anjou and the Dukes of Brittany fought bitterly. The remains of the château look down over the Loire.

Coudray-Montbault

The Château of Coudray-Montbault, which is surrounded by moats of flowing water, illustrates the primordial importance, for the 15th and 16th centuries, of decorative detail. While some designers relied on the interplay of stonework of different colors, here the pink brick has been enhanced with a pattern of dark green lozenges of enameled brick. Two round towers frame the dwelling, to which access is provided by a stone bridge built to replace the drawbridge, while a third tower forms an angle towards the rear. The ruins of the 12th-century church and the 13th-century priory can be seen at the end of the French gardens, while the contemporary chapel contains a fine life-size sculpture of Christ being laid in the tomb.

The two joined towers of the Château of Champtoceaux (1). Chanzeaux (2). Coudray-Montbault (3).

1△

2▽

the entrance are the château's most attractive adornments. An unusual structure with pointed pediments stands next to the chapel, its cut-off corners making it look somewhat like a dovecote. It is the staircase tower leading to the seigniorial dwelling.

These delicate architectural features contrast starkly with the outer face of Le Plessis-Macé, which consists of a surrounding wall with towers and a rectangular medieval keep, all of which are only slightly dilapidated.

Durtal

From the covered way of this large, six-storey keep whose walls are built of alternating layers of schist and limestone, it is possible to admire the charming town on the banks of the Loir. It is a view which Henri II and Catherine de Médicis or Charles IX, as guests in these pepper-pot towers, must certainly have relished. For the most part, however, the Château of Durtal belongs to the style of Louis XIII; a noble residence with slender skylights looks down over the courtyard, with its elegant cabled colonnettes.

La Tremblaye

The Château of La Tremblaye, situated near a small lake not far from Cholet, brings to mind the gentleman-poet who went to see Voltaire at Ferney; after his visit a few letters from the philosopher quite turned his head, and ruined his career.

Le Plessis-Macé (1). The châteaux of Durtal (2) and La Tremblaye, at Cholet (3).

3 ▽

Le Plessis-Macé

Louis XI stayed at this château built by his chamberlain Louis de Beaumont in the 11th-century fortress founded by Macé du Plessis, a local feudal lord. This magnificent residence marks the transition between two eras; and after Louis XI, three other monarchs – Charles VIII, François I and Henry IV – enjoyed staying there, although by then it had changed owners, and belonged to the Du Bellay family. It was they who were responsible for the construction of the chapel, with its finely sculpted accolade doorway and its 15th-century altar; another of its interesting features is the two-storey gallery of carved wood, one level of which was for the masters and the other for visitors.

The same upstairs/downstairs division occurs in the arrangements made for watching the frequent festivities in the courtyard, such as jousting, receptions or jugglers. In this case, however, the servants' balcony was on the same side as the outbuildings, while that reserved for the lord of the manor was in the corner of the dwelling itself; this is the gem of Le Plessis-Macé. Whereas the walls of the building consist of dark schist alternating with clamps of tuff, only the more malleable white stone was used to make the princely loggia. The fine sculptures above

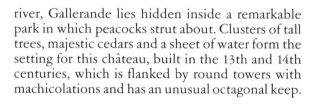

Bazouges

This charming complex, consisting of a château, its seigniorial mill on the Loir and a park in the French style surrounded by water, was the work of Baudouin de Champagne, the chamberlain of Louis XII and François I. The two stout white towers with machicolations and pepper-pots were added later; one of them houses the chapel, whose ceiling is vaulted in the Angevin style, that is, almost in the form of a cupola.

Courtanvaux

A succession of families owned the Château of Courtanvaux, the seat of a marquisate — the Souvré, Louvois (including Louis XIV's Minister of War) and Montesquiou Fezensac, the family of the "true d'Artagnan", marshal of France. After being abandoned for many years, the château was revived in 1811, when the Countess of Montesquiou, the governess of the King of Rome, settled there with the "young eagle".

Poncé

During the Renaissance, the feudal castle of the lords of Poncé was replaced by this harmonious dwelling, which has one of the finest staircases to be seen anywhere. It consists of six straight flights, two per floor; each of the 135 white stone coffer vaults above it contains a different sculpted theme — plant, animal or human — of matchless artistry.

Craon

At Craon the Toulouse architect Pommeyrol built a typically Louis XVI château, while the profusion of garlands, vases, medallions and masks which enhance the façade were the work of the sculptor Lemeunier. The English park, from the Romantic period, was designed by Chatelain; a garden in the French style lies deep within it.

Gallerande

Slightly upstream from Bazouges, but far from the river, Gallerande lies hidden inside a remarkable park in which peacocks strut about. Clusters of tall trees, majestic cedars and a sheet of water form the setting for this château, built in the 13th and 14th centuries, which is flanked by round towers with machicolations and has an unusual octagonal keep.

Laval

The oldest part of the Château of Laval is also the most extraordinary: the keep, built in the early part of the 12th century, has retained not only its original roof, but also its beams, which extend over the walls to form the hoarding. Huge radiating beams rest on the masonry, the weight of the hoarding being counter-balanced by the mass of a monumental central crown-post.

The Château of Bazouges-sur-le-Loir (1). Poncé (2). Courtanvaux (3). Gallerande (4). Craon (5). *Last page:* the Château of Laval.

Credits:

Arthaud 107 — Bénazet 1, 2c, 3b, 4a, b, c, 5a, 8b, c, 9, 10c, 22a, b, 26b, c, d, 36a, 37a, 38a, b, 40a, b, c, d, 41, 43, 46c, d, 48, 50c, d, 52c, 53c, 61c, 66a, b, 67a, b, 68a, 69, 70b, 72b, 73, 81b, 82, 84-85, 90a, b, 93a, b, c, d, f, 95, 98a, 99, 105, 110a, 113b, 114a, b, c, d, 120a, b, 121a, b, c, 122a, b, 123a, b, 124c, 125a, b, c, 127a, 128a, b, c, 129a, b, c, 130b, d, 132a, 133a, b, c, 134a, b, 135a, b, 136a, 138a, 140a, b, 143a, b — Cauchetier 2b, 20a — La Cigogne 112, 124b, 126b, 142, 143c, 144 — Delon 115 — Dichter-Lourie 124a — Gaud 36b, 37b — Gontscharoff 49b, 56a — Halary 57b — Labbé 42b, 44c, 130a, c, 131, 143d — De Laubier 39a, b — List 5b, 97a, 102a — Meauxsoone 34-35 — Perdereau 100a, 119b — Pix gardes, 2a, 6a, b, c, d, 8a, 10a, b, 12a, b, 13a, b, 14, 15a, b, 16a, b, 17b, 18-19, 20b, 21, 23, 24a, b, 25a, b, c, 26a, 27, 28a, b, 29a, b, 30-31, 32c, 33, 36c, 42a, c, 44a, b, 45, 46a, b, 47a, b, 49a, 50a, b, 51a, b, 52a, b, 53a, b, d, e, 54-55, 56c, 57a, 58, 59, 60a, b, c, d, e, 61a, b, 62-63, 64a, b, 65a, b, 68b, 70a, c, 71b, c, 72a, 74, 75a, b, c, 77, 78a, b, 79, 80a, b, c, 81a, 83, 86a, b, c, 87a, b, c, d, 88-89, 90c, d, 91, 92b, 93e, 94a, b, c, 96a, b, 97b, c, 101a, b, 102b, 103a, b, 104a, b, 106a, b, c, d, 108-109, 110b, 111, 113a, c, 116a, b, 117, 127b, 134c, 137b, 139 — Planchard 92a, 98b, 136b — Revault 3a, 7, 16c, 17a, 100b, 101c, 103c, 118a, b, c, 119a, 137a, 138b, 141 — Riby 32a, 56b, 71a, 76, 126a.

All the pictures by
    "L'AGENCE/PIX—PARIS,,